GIVING
THE
PERFECT
GIFT

Sandra Wilson

Published by
Hara Publishing
P.O. Box 19732
Seattle, WA 98109

ISBN: 1-883697-49-2
Library of Congress Number: 95-094788

DEDICATION

To the generous and thoughtful Gift
Givers who have touched my world.

ACKNOWLEDGEMENT

Some of the most enjoyable time on this book was spent talking to friends, to relatives, and to fellow passengers about memorable gifts. I thank all of you for sharing what was important to you. We were talking about more than gifts, weren't we?

Thank you Sheryn Hara, Margaret Smith, Brook Blumenstein, and Ron DeWilde for the gift of creating a book from my collection of ideas and loose typed pages.

TABLE OF CONTENTS

INTRODUCTION

Q: What do birthdays, anniversaries, Hanukkah, Christmas, and Valentine's Day have in common?

A: They are all gift-giving opportunities.

Q: What do you have occasion to do several times a year?

A: Give gifts.

Q: What is a thoughtful gesture to make when you visit a home for the first time?

A: Bring a gift.

Q: What can you do when you find or make something perfect for a friend?

A: Give it as a gift.

Q: What is one way of showing that someone means a lot to you?

A: Give a gift.

Giving and receiving gifts is a part of your life. This book will help you create a personal "gift-giving place" full of fun, anticipation, and good feelings.

To start, bring to mind a particular gift you received that was more important to you than others. Because its memory has lasted, it is probable that this gift captured something valuable and important about you.

You can create this same magic for another. When you combine the ideas and the guidelines in this book with

your own intuition and talents, you will quickly become known as a champion gift giver.

The pages of this book are for you to read and for you to write upon. The wide margins are an invitation to you to jot down your personal notes and comments. There are specific, titled spaces throughout the book for your thoughts, but you don't have to wait or stop to look for them when you have something worth writing down RIGHT NOW!

An idea for someone? Jot it down. Circle important words. Use your highlighter. Write questions in the margins. Act when the inspiration or the question comes to mind. Know that as you interact with the printed words, you are creating your own unique and personal book.

Giving the Perfect Gift is, at best, a source of ideas, the beginning of your brainstorms. As the reader, you alone can breathe life into the possibilities on these pages.

Relish a gift that was memorable to you. Give to someone with originality and vision. Share this process with me and subsequently with others through the pages of my next gift-giving book. I look forward to hearing from you.

Sandra Wilson

IS THIS BOOK FOR YOU?

Yes, If :

★ you can tell that your giftees are not delighted with their presents.

★ you never see your gifts worn or used.

★ gift giving fills you with dread, rather than enthusiasm.

★ giving special gifts is important to you.

★ you are a Champion Gift Giver and are always on the lookout for new inspiration.

Use this book as a guide to help you explore new gift-giving territory. As you

read this book, you'll find some quotes from various gift-givers and giftees, some questions to ask yourself about gift-giving options, and some space to jot notes for those occasions when you need to find the Perfect Gift.

2

WHAT IS A PERFECT GIFT?

As the giver of a gift, you can only hope and guess that what you give will be appropriate for each person. Only the receiver of your gift will *know* if it is perfect. The gift may be tangible or intangible. Store-bought or hand-made. Expensive or not. Quick or time-consuming to assemble. Some of the best gifts of all are crafted by unskilled but loving hands.

The Perfect Gift is different for each person. One recipient's "Ho hum" is another's "Yippee!" A Perfect Gift expresses the idea that you honor an important part of the person who receives the gift. It may fill a need. It may delight a fancy. It always says that

you have paid attention, observed, been aware, and discovered that person's wants or needs. You care.

4

WHEN SHOULD YOU GIVE A GIFT?

Some gifts are given at expected times, such as birthdays, weddings, Christmas, Hanukkah, and Valentine's Day.

Others are given for your very own reasons, such as:

- ★ "I Love You"
- ★ "It's Wednesday"
- ★ "It's Favorite Aunt Day"
- ★ "Thanks for Everything"
- ★ "I Want To"

What are some other special occasions you'd like to celebrate by giving gifts?

SURVEY

Perfection, like beauty, is in the eye and heart of the beholder. The questions below, to ask yourself *before* giving, will help you focus on your giftees and will reveal what each considers to be a Perfect Gift—the kind you want to give.

★ What is important to your giftees?
What are they passionate about?

★ How do they spend their free time?

★ What are their favorite foods?

★ What are their fashion preferences?
What are their *correct* sizes?

7

★What do they collect? What motifs and symbols do they prefer?

★What sports are they wild about? Which team do they root for?

★How can you make the presentation memorable?

Are there other questions you might ask about your giftees?

Now you are ready to use the following ideas to zero in on a gift that will be given with pleasure and received with excitement.

A COMMENT ON MEN AND GIFTS

Much of this book seems geared toward women as buyers, presenters, and receivers of gifts. The word "gift" seems to

8

be more personal to women. Perhaps they are more comfortable with the whole idea of giving.

When asked about a special gift, most of the women, as well as a few of the men, would respond, often with more than one memory. Effort, thought, and a "piece" of the giver seemed to touch women more deeply than men.

This book will help men understand what a woman sees as a Perfect Gift. It will expand a woman's own awareness and depth of knowledge.

Inquiries suggest that men enjoy receiving gifts that let them know they are important to the giver. They can, however, get this feeling more simply than a woman may. In general, men are satisfied and even delighted with

9

more practical gifts. Many men love to get gifts that plug in. Gadgets. The latest toy. While ideas in this book are appropriate for both sexes, "The Nitty Gritty of Gift Giving" section at the back of this book focuses on hobbies, motifs, and interests that are especially appropriate when shopping for a man.

10

TANGLES TO AVOID

Champion gift-givers know that as well as Perfect Gifts, there are some sure-fire *Imperfect* Gifts! Steer clear of these tangles:

★ **As a rule, women don't like to get gifts that plug in.**
No toasters, no blenders, and no electric knives. Exceptions include gourmet kitchen items like espresso machines. If you need a plug-in item, get it. Just don't count it as her gift!

★**Never ask, "What would you like for your birthday?" the day before the birthday.**

It is a dead giveaway that you have not done anything in advance. People have been known to make assumptions about their sense of worth to you by noticing the lead time you give yourself to get their gifts.

★ **Keep your gift appropriate for *the receiver* and not for you.**

Give something the person wants to receive rather than something that you want to give. When you give people candy or flowers or anything else, give them *their* favorites, not yours.

"I opened my gift for Valentine's Day and my husband had given me a box of candy—his favorite. Who was he thinking of when he gave it to me? I was so mad, I threw it. He realized what he had done and came back later with something for me."

12

★ **Neither cash nor gift certificates should be given in a straightforward way, such as in an envelope or cash card.**

If cash or a certificate is your choice, then put your effort into making the presentation exciting. Buy a CD and present it with a certificate for more CDs, tape $1 bills all over a framed mirror, or stack the bills neatly and wrap them up for a great surprise.

★ **Your gift should be personal, unless your relationship is outside this area.**

A scarf or a shirt is usually more welcomed than a savings bond.

"All my life I have been receiving practical gifts. I appreciated them, because we were often on a limited budget. Now that I am a grandmother, I feel sad that I have trained people to see me only as a practical person. So I was delighted one birthday to

13

receive a perfectly charming—and totally useless!—teddy bear. I proudly display it in my living room."

★ As a rule, women do not get excited about practical gifts.

Men are more likely to. To be safe, present something that appeals to a woman's heart more than to her head.

"On Mother's Day, my husband presented me with a trio of wrapped gifts. We dressed up our children, took the wrapped gifts with us, and went out to a restaurant. My gifts turned out to be a shoe rack ("So you can straighten out the bottom of your closet,") a glass canister ("I thought this would be good for you to put flour in,") and a cutting board ("I saw this demonstrated and it looked great."). His gifts said to me that he thought of me as his messy, live-in cook. My head knew that this was not the truth, but neither my heart nor my womanhood were touched by these presents."

14

★ **If you want your giftees to try something out of character, ask them to try it another time, not during gift time.**

Present something that is consistent with what they do, what they wear, and who they are now. Gifts should reflect the feeling that you have seen this person in a true light, and you understand and accept that person for who he or she is.

"I saw a tie in the store window that I just loved and wanted to get it for my boyfriend. The only thing was, I had never seen him in anything as splashy and bold as that tie. All of his other clothes were conservative. I love him the way he is, and if I can encourage him to loosen up with his print and color selection, I can do that another time, not on Christmas morning. My thinking was, if I bought the tie, he would think I was not paying attention to him, or that I would want him to be different than he

15

is, or that I prefer my taste over his. None of that is true."

"My boyfriend just bought me a wonderful pair of earrings. They are a great color and design. The only thing wrong with them is that they are for pierced ears. I wonder, has he never noticed that I don't have holes in my earlobes?"

★ Don't guess on sizes!

Know current sizes. (You can fill out and carry the Size Chart found in the back of this book.) Remember that shopping excursion when you held up a dress to a total stranger, hoping that she was the same size as your mother? Perhaps you have been that stranger! While it is a charming way to meet people, it does reflect a certain lack of knowledge about the person, who is, after all, important enough to warrant a gift.

16

A size chart is worth its weight in gold. And before you buy fashion gifts, there are questions to ask: Does she like to wear blouses alone or under jackets? Does he prefer his pants pleated or not? These are questions that will load you up with helpful information before you walk into a department store.

Fashion questions, sizes and more are covered in the "Nitty Gritty" section in the back of this book.

17

A DOZEN PERFECT GIFT IDEAS

Browse through the following ideas, keeping a certain gift recipient in mind. Which idea is just perfect? Which would be perfect with a slight adaptation?

Gift Idea 1: Motifs

What motifs or symbols are important to this special person—irises, frogs, or stars? Fish, suns, penguins, or *Gone with the Wind* memorabilia?

19

Look for these motifs and buy them with that certain someone in mind.

"I love stars. One birthday, I received star-emblazoned anklets, a star photograph frame, star soap, a star drawer pull, star note cards, and a journal with stars on the cover."

Keeping up to date on preferences helps. One woman collected cows for years, but she finally grew tired of them. You wouldn't want to be the next person to give her a cow-shaped clock.

Gift Idea 2: Sports
Is this person a sports enthusiast? Clothing or equipment dealing with the sport may be appropriate. The sport as a motif can extend to items that have a bicycle, running shoes, golf balls, or a tennis racket on them. Other sport-related gifts include sport lessons or tickets to special events.

20

"I like to camp. I'm always looking for new and useful gadgets to use outdoors. I found a flashlight that could convert into a stand-up lantern. My handyman father appreciated it when I presented him with it."

Gift Idea 3: Tickets

Consider tickets to a musical concert. The museum. A play. A wood-carver show. The circus. A movie festival. A favorite performer's show in town. To add the crowning touch, include a written invitation to dinner or lunch.

"A Christmas gift my wife and I remember fondly is a present from our daughter and son-in-law. The gift included a pair of tickets to see a stage show that was coming to town, as well as a tape of the music. In addition, they took us out to dinner before the event and made it an evening to remember."

Gift Idea 4: Dream

Fulfill a dream. A trip to Disneyland. A day at the circus. The birthday party they should have had when they were seven and still talk about wistfully.

"I knew again that I was in love for the long run when my husband gave me several months of tap dancing lessons. He had listened and remembered when I shared memories of how, years ago, I wanted to tap dance so much that I would visit my childhood friend and practice with her after each of her lessons. Now I have my own lessons."

Gift Idea 5: Tuition

Give someone the tuition to take a class. Consider one that you would enjoy taking together. Look through course catalogues of community schools in your area and consider learning to photograph mountain goats. Prepare Indian food. Grow an herb garden. Defend yourself with martial arts.

22

Stay afloat in a kayak. Create helpful compost. Live frugally in Paris.

"My wife and I were both intrigued with handwriting analysis, so we took a course in it. This became a shared interest on a hobby level, and it was one more topic that we had in common."

Gift Idea 6: Food

Prepare or present to your giftees a meal of their personal favorites. Forget the basic food groups, and enjoy Fettucini Alfredo, Beef Wellington, and a chocolate soufflé—all in one splurge. You cannot get gout from a single meal! Your gastronomic kindness will be fondly remembered.

"On Mother's Day I received an abundance of favorite things from my son and husband. My breakfast in bed included fresh apricots, fresh raspberries, a croissant, and champagne. To top it all off, they left me alone for two hours to read my favorite book in

23

bed and drink champagne. I still remember it fondly."

How might you be able to combine favorite foods with a gift?

Gift Idea 7: Presentation

Provide extra gift pleasure with a dazzling presentation. Gifts that are boxed, boxes that are wrapped, and wrapping that is ribboned, all add their singular impact, increasing the value and thoughtfulness of the gift. Multi-colored cellophane, sparkles, and fancy ribbons offer the giftee a treasure hunt to find the item inside. Place stamps, stickers, or photos on the tags or the giftwrap.

24

"My husband bought me a piece of jewelry for Christmas. To add to the suspense, and to let me know that this gift blew the budget (not only for Christmas but for Valentine's Day, Fourth of July, Secretary's Day, St. Patrick's Day, Halloween, Mother's Day, and my birthday), he combed the storerooms of card shops to find cards for each of those occasions. He presented the cards to me throughout Christmas morning before I finally received my diamonds. What a kick! It must have taken him hours of effort getting those cards."

"My wife bought me a special table, which came in two parts. The round glass top was in a large, flat box. The stand was in a large triangle-shaped box. Wrapped together and tied with an appropriately-large bow, the ensemble was huge. She put it beside the tree and attached a giant tag, which said the gift was for her. Then she called me at work, all excited about this monster

25

present that I had supposedly delivered on our porch. I 'fessed up to not knowing what it was. We 'both' tried to guess who had given it to her. Finally it was revealed on Christmas morning that it was for ME. I finally got all the details of the caper. The table was just right. The presentation was memorable."

Gift Idea 8: Baskets

Gather a basketful of items linked to this person's favorite hobby, collection, or motif. Everything within this basket (or other container) could be related. If it is a birthday gift, include a small present for every year. Professional gift basket companies can help you come up with novel ideas that focus on a regional theme, a celebration theme, or a company theme. Or just use your imagination. Pack your presents into a tool box for the handy-person. For the artist, fill a ceramic vase with brushes, paint tubes, and other supplies. For the

26

gourmet cook, fill a salad bowl with vegetable seeds or herb starts.

From the gifter: *"I wanted to prepare a special gift for a friend who was celebrating a significant birthday. I created a small booklet filled with a page for each year. On each page, I pasted a picture of something that reminded me specially of her. An accompanying basket included ribboned items, such as a cassette tape, a small photo frame, a sack of gourmet coffee, a pouch for herbs, and so on."*

From the giftee: *"Sue's gift was such fun to open. We sat down together and went over each page of the booklet. I opened all of the items in the beautifully ribboned basket. It was touching to know how much of me she had seen. The basket has been well used, and I still have the booklet. I won't ever forget how the impact of the total gift was much more than the individual items in the basket."*

Gift Idea 9: Photographs

Almost no gift is more personal than a framed portrait, no matter how formal or informal it is. Frame a favorite picture of this person, or a picture of you with this person. Or simply present a frame with a certificate inside for a professional photo session—a glamour shot that includes a makeover and a variety of outfits to choose from. Find a specialty frame. Make a collage of photos. Put together a personalized photo album.

"My girlfriend gave me a large picture frame shaped like a fish. Inside this frame was a collection of photos of a fishing trip I took with my brother and nephew. She collected the photos and cut them to fit the spaces within the frame. Now, thanks to her, I have a lasting momento of a special time."

"Our dog is just like part of the family. Perhaps that is why we were so tickled to get this gift from our friends: they had arranged dog biscuits on a frame and

28

spray painted it. Inside the frame was a photo of our dog."

"My wife and I have always taken movies of our family, from the time the children were very young. Even though we love these nostalgic movies, they were taken on reel-to-reel film and required a cumbersome and noisy projector to run them. Last Christmas, one of the children had the film transferred to a video tape. Music was added, the blank spaces were removed, and there were captions at the beginning and end of this precious footage of our Early Years. Not only that, but the video does not take up much space. At our age, that's important."

29

Gift Idea 10: Togetherness

Give a gift that involves doing something (maybe together) after the day of gift giving. This can be set up so that your gift is also a gift of attention to their needs.

"Our son pleased us when he bought a gallon of paint and brushes with a note saying that he would be over to paint the dining room on Tuesday. We finished a task we had been planning. As a bonus, we enjoyed the evening we spent with him."

"I loved it when my girlfriend selected four things from a shop that I like. She instructed me to go to this shop and ask for Terry. Terry pulled out four items that my girlfriend had already preselected, and I got to pick my favorite. My girlfriend had already done the shopping and selecting, and I had the fun of choosing the one very best gift. She had, of course, already prearranged pay-

30

ment with Terry, so I got to take the gift and smilingly walk away."

"My sister created a culinary masterpiece out of her very own kitchen. It wasn't something easy or natural for her to do. Because of this, I was even more pleased with the gift."

"My granddaughter stopped by the other day with a wonderful gift for me. She knows that I like to serve a fresh cookie with tea or coffee when I have guests. But having the materials on hand and putting together the cookies that I used to bake all the time is harder and harder for me. What she did for me was very thoughtful: she prepared a double batch of cookie dough, packaged it into small containers and tucked them into my freezer. Now when I have guests, I simply bake the cookies from the dough that is waiting for me."

31

Gift Idea 11: Quality

When you are on a limited budget, seriously consider buying one wonderful item, rather than two or more items of lesser value. Go for quality before quantity. This principle is handy when buying jewelry, tools, ties, stationery—just about anything.

"Friends came over to celebrate our anniversary when all four of us were budget-conscious. They told us they wanted to bring the steaks for dinner. Instead of buying four large T-bones, they bought four smaller and tastier tenderloins. A touch of class. Their gift included the rest of the meal, preparation, and even cleanup."

Gift Idea 12: Ingredients

Present a gift of many ingredients. This idea is not only a gift but an event, a happening. Give a recipe with the right pan and the non-perishable ingredients. Video tapes

32

with popcorn. Hiking boots with a book about local hikes. Soup mix packaged into separate soup mugs (with directions, of course).

"My brother drinks martinis. Since I don't, when he visited, we had to make do to prepare his favorite drink. The following Christmas, I was delighted to receive from him four martini glasses and bottles of gin, vermouth, and olives. He provided something I don't normally have to offer my guests."

CATALOGUE GIVING

Just about every day, catalogues appear in your mailbox. These catalogues feature the most amazing assortment of merchandise. They come without your request. Perhaps you treat them as trash and throw them away as soon as you receive them. Perhaps you put them on the growing stack of "things to read when I have time." Perhaps they weigh on your mind as something you should do *something* about.

While the bad news is that these catalogues arrive endlessly, silently, and demandingly, there is good news. The good news is that these same mailings can be put to a use even better than filling your recycling container.

You need to give gifts. You receive quantities of catalogues. Let these two situations work together: use your catalogues to give gifts that are memorable and perfect.

Reasons to Shop with Catalogues

★**Time.** With catalogues, you can shop in the comfort of your own home. You can go through the pages with someone in mind, make a list of ideas, and pick the very best one without having to back-track to another store. You can take small snatches of your time here and there. Compare the time you would spend catalogue shopping with the time you would spend driving to the store, parking, walking, shopping, waiting in lines, then driving home. Catalogues can save you time.

★**Ideas.** In a catalogue you are able to look at items singly, which can be

36

advantageous. In a store, you might choose a gift simply because it looked great in an artfully arranged display. Reading through a catalogue, you can take the time to examine items and their functions, studying the accompanying descriptions. Just seeing all of the items displayed on the pages gives you an opportunity to brainstorm. These catalogues can be looked upon as a dynamic source of possibly perfect ideas that you may have otherwise missed.

"As soon as I saw the ladybug wrist-watch in the catalogue, I knew that I had to order it for my daughter-in-law, who has a collection of ladybug designs."

★**Style.** If you don't regularly spend time in retail stores, it is easy to fall behind the merchandising and fashion curve, not knowing what is hot this season, what's cold from last season.

37

Catalogues bring you direct news from the latest buying frontiers. They all want to be the first to show you what is happening this year.

★**Depth.** In recent years, catalogue companies have gone far in offering products related to a particular subject or interest. Can you match this to an interest of your giftee? Reading. Photography. Golf. Popcorn. Home furnishings. Cigars. Spas. Pets. They all have at least one catalogue dedicated to them.

★**Returns.** It doesn't fit? It doesn't look like it did in the catalogue? Found something else? Changed your mind? Send it back. Most catalogues have open return policies; they know they won't please all of the people all of the time. If you use catalogues much, you will soon discover those that match your personality and offer the very best return service. Save the box your order

38

arrived in. If necessary, you can use it for returns. You return things to stores, don't you? You try on clothes that you *think* will be great but aren't, don't you? Catalogues simply allow you to do this in your own home. Most catalogue companies deal with a "satisfaction or your money back" guarantee.

★**Ease.** To place an order, you call a 1-800 number. Your call will probably be answered by a well-trained person sitting by a computer loaded with information about catalogue items. That operator will take the important information from you and will write your order. You will get an order number, the total cost of the order, and approximate shipping date. If the information is not forthcoming automatically, ask for it. It is there.

Want to save yourself another step when you are certain you have the right item? Ask the catalogue company to

giftwrap and mail the item to the intended person. Tell them what they should write on the enclosed card.

Reasons You Might *Not* Want to Shop with a Catalogue for Gifts

★ **Different.** You have never thought about using catalogues before and you are not certain that you will like it. Catalogue ordering is out of your comfort zone and you would rather not try something that you are not familiar with. You have always shopped at a particular mall or in a certain town. What if you don't like it? What if it doesn't fit?

★ **Not My Idea.** Perhaps you have a general dislike of being involved with something that you did not initiate. It is true that these catalogues keep coming to your home on a very regular and hefty basis, even though

40

you never asked for them. You will receive catalogues, whether you request them or not.

You can always fall back on the idea that you are not required to read something that was mailed to you just because it has your name on it. If you feel uncomfortable or angry with the catalogue company, you can always dump the darn thing in the recycle bin.

★**More and More.** If you think that you get a lot of catalogues now, just order from one, and it seems as though you are on everyone's list. Keep an open outlook; realize that you would indeed have a charmed life if this were the worst thing that happened to you.

★**Reduced Personal Involvement.** If you truly love shopping, handling the merchandise before you buy, chatting with other shoppers, and carrying packages around, you will miss that if

41

you shop through catalogues. Perhaps you could split the shopping between pages and stores.

Using Your Catalogue Creatively

There are ways to *use* catalogues, beyond looking at the pages and ordering what you want. They can be a fertile source of ideas, a way of getting to know someone.

★**Questions and Answers.** Look at a catalogue page with a friend. Decide silently what you think the other person would like the best on that page. Ask and listen to the answer. You might have been absolutely right. If you weren't right, you might learn from your friend's choice and comments.

Ask questions such as: "If you could own any one thing from this page, what would it be?" Listen to not only the *what* but the *why*. Did either of you choose

42

differently than you would have a year ago? You can learn about others this way, regardless of whether you are amazingly perceptive or surprised by their answers.

This is a quick, non-threatening exchange that can open your eyes to the preferences of another and give you ideas for future gift giving.

★**Distance Shopping.** Send a catalogue to people who are far away or whose taste is unknown to you. Brothers-in-law. Aunts. Children of good friends. Have them mark as many items in the catalogue as they would like. Ask them to indicate preferred sizes and colors, as well. When you get the returned catalogue, you can select your gift from the marked items. That way, they will still be surprised and you can still stay within your budget. Most importantly, you will know that you have sent them something they will undoubtedly enjoy.

43

★**Hobby Shopping.** Do you know someone who has a specific hobby? Catalogues can help you find something special. However, if you see pages and pages of items that deal with archery, you might wonder what the perfect archery gift would be. Consider sending this archer the entire catalogue. Let him or her mark several items and send it back to you. With great relief you can order from the preferred items knowing not only will what you get will be appropriate, but it will also be the right size and it won't be a duplicate.

★ **Personal Favorites.** Consider using catalogues to get what *you* want to get. Recognize that buying for you is sometimes a tricky situation for others. Help them out by marking items in catalogues that fit both your style and all budgets. Place this catalogue in an obvious spot before gift time so that they will have time to look it over and

44

make their selections. If people are going to spend money on you, you will be particularly delighted if they spend money on a gift that you really want or know you can use. They will be happy too.

★**Funded Certificates.** Perhaps you will use a catalogue slightly differently and attach a check made out to the catalogue company itself. Send both items to someone on your list with a note saying, in one way or another, "You choose."

★**Particular Giftees.** Young people are among those who have very explicit ideas of what they will or won't wear. They used to love T-shirts and sweatshirts. Now they may have expanded their tastes. Perhaps they have accumulated so much casual wear that they'd rather have something else. Catalogues are better than your guesses. Send them appropriate catalogues, and ask them to mark sizes and colors of

45

everything they like. You have a sure-fire gift list from this. All you have to do is decide your budget category and make the 1-800 phone call.

46

WRAPPING

Gifts that are wrapped carry additional punch and sparkle. There are many possibilities that add to the value of the gift without adding much expense. The ideas below are here for you to use for wrapping or as a source of related ideas. Have fun! If the idea of wrapping ties you in knots, however, forget it and have a professional put your package together.

★**Containers.** Baskets. Suitcases. Canisters. Stockings. Tool boxes. Tubes. Flower pots. Casserole dishes. Milk cartons. Cans of all sorts. Drawers. Jars. Gift bags. Buckets. Bird cages. Water-

ing cans. Boxes of all sizes. Mailing pouches. Bottles. Laundry bags.

What else comes to your mind?

★**Gift Wrap.** Tissue paper. Wallpaper. Posters. Fabric. Purchased wrapping paper. Maps. Cellophane paper. Brown bags. Towels. Paper that has been copied with photos of the giver or the receiver. Newspaper (comics? financial section?). Try making your own wrap on butcher paper with stamps and stencils, hand or fingerprints, potato or block print.

What else?

48

★**Ribbon.** Tinsel. Multi-colored ribbon. Raffia. Foil. Elastic. Jute. String. Wired.

Other ideas?

★**Decorations.** Feathers. Paper dolls. Paper fans. Glitter. Stickers. Doilies. Lace. Fresh herbs. Paper fans. Sequins. Cake decorations. Mylar balloons. Curled paper strips. Balloons. Stencils. Candy. Seashells. Pasta. Cinnamon sticks. Drawings. Cut designs (snowflakes, etc.). Flowers (real, paper, silk). Rubber stamps. Money (coins and bills). Collages (pictures, photographs, gift wrap). Paper pocket holding a special secret. Bows of many colors, sizes, and materials.

What are your ideas?

★**Signature Wrap.** Always wrap your gifts with at least one constant factor that is yours alone. The exterior of your packages will be recognized by everyone because you always use distinctive brown wrapping paper with gold ribbon, you always adhere your personal adhesive seal, you always attach a particular flower in the bow, always use ribbon with your name on it...

★**Store Wrapping.** Professional, dazzling, store wrapping. This is what you use when you have more money than time, or when you admit that your own lack of dexterity and supplies will make store wrapping a better choice. Many gift givers are glad to present something beautifully wrapped from the store.

★**Related Gifts.** Attach a small or related item to the outside of your gift for extra flair. Children (and the child in adults) love this. Use a headband, pin, perfume, kitchen gadget, corkscrew,

seed packet, cosmetics, and small books to hint at the surprise inside.

PRESENTATION

What does your gift say before it is opened? You can choose to make your presentation, your first message, memorable and heartfelt. Your feelings about the person, the occasion, and your gift are communicated, even if they are not spoken.

It is easy to forget that the presentation of your gift can boost its value and memory power a great deal. Gifts handed to the receiver unwrapped or in a brown bag speak of something unimportant to the person giving the gift. If the gift is worth giving, it is worth giving with flair. So, where do you find flair?

53

The packaging and presentation of your gifts say something about you. You can determine this message. Choose from these ideas to create something you want to communicate:

★Give a clue card instead of the gift. This card leads the receiver to a particular spot where there is another clue card waiting. Continue until the gift is found. Poets can make their cards rhyme.

★Tie a long string to the gift, weave the string throughout the area and give the loose end to the receiver to follow to the surprise.

★For something BIG, put a bow on it and leave it outside. Blindfold the receiver and take him or her to where the gift will be seen as soon as the blindfold is removed. This works well for cars, boats, bicycles, large yard sculptures, trees, golf carts, and snowmobiles.

54

★Arrange for friends or neighbors to keep the gift for you. Consider asking them to deliver the gift, ring the bell, then quickly leave. Or, let them be part of the presentation.

★Ask your waiter or maitre d' to deliver the gift to your restaurant table.

★Place your gift in a special spot, and devise a reason for both of you to go to that spot. Let the person know that there is something in the hollow tree trunk, in the office, along the creek...

"One Christmas my husband wrapped a box of sand. Inside the sand was a toy chaise lounge, a bottle of sun tan lotion, a pair of sunglasses, and two tickets to Hawaii!"

"My husband took me away for the weekend. He told me by putting a series of footsteps on the floor for me to follow when I came in the door. The footsteps led to my open suitcase."

★If you are going to be present when the gift is open, think about what you would like to say to this person. If you mumble or say nothing, you lose an opportunity to reach out to someone who is important enough in your life to receive a gift from you.

Let your giftees know that you have thought about them in choosing this gift. You are giving them something that you think will have special meaning for them.

What was *your* favorite gift presentation? (It may be a gift that you gave or received.) What specifically made it memorable for you? What are some new ideas you have for presenting a gift?

56

MEMORABLE GIFTS

Here are some wonderful responses to the question, "What was your most memorable gift?"

Receiving

★**A letter from my daughter.** As a mother, I knew all of the things I would have liked to have done differently. But my daughter told me all of the things that I have done right. This letter told me that although she will always be my little princess, she no longer needed to see things in her world from the vantage point of a princess. The letter is tucked in my box of special treasures.

57

★**Bath.** When I was a single mom, I came home tired from a tough day at work. My children sensed my fatigue and drew me a bath with bubbles, flowers, wine, and lighted candles. They had me sit and soak in the bathtub while they did the dishes. Their gift to me was seeing my need and acting upon it, without my even thinking of it.

★**Diamond earrings.** I had never had anything that nice before. They were the nicest thing I had ever been given.

★**Tickets.** A friend picked me up when I arrived at the local airport. It was my birthday. Between the two front seats sat a stuffed penguin my friend had made for me. Even more special was a pair of tickets for a show that we were going to see together in a nearby town.

★**Candlesticks.** I saw pair of candlesticks in a store window and mentioned

to my friend that they were about the only thing I liked in there. Later, my friend showed up with these same candlesticks in his hand for me.

★**Grandparents.** My grandparents allowed me to be different. I particularly remember being given a bicycle for Christmas; because it was too wintry to ride the bike outside, my grandmother let me ride it inside her house, around and around. This same grandmother would spend hours with me on rainy days in front of their imitation fireplace in a tent, imagining being in other places.

★ **Lobster pot.** When my husband and I bought a home, we decided to have a nautical theme in the decorating. My parents figured that a lobster pot would be just the thing to have. When they took a trip to Newfoundland, they searched for one. They rented a car; they drove to out-of-the-way places; they talked with people that they never

59

would have, had they not been on this quest. Because it was lobster season, all the pots were being used. After much searching, they talked to an old fisherman who said that all of his new pots were being used, but asked, "Did you want an old one?" This was perfect. They went to his house and dug it out of a pile of discards. The fisherman did not want any money because he knew that they would have enough trouble trying to get the bulky thing back on the plane. This lobster pot is now in a place of prominence in my home. I can't decide if the pot or the story was the better gift.

★**Surprises.** My favorite gifts have had the element of surprise about them. On a birthday, the man I was dating had arranged for a choir at a concert to sing "Happy Birthday" to me, in front of the entire audience! This same man surprised me with a short and totally wonderful cruise. No "reason" for that gift.

60

★**Small remembrances.** My 12-year-old granddaughter stops by a store to buy small things for me. I love them, because she does not have to do this, and she buys things I really enjoy. She has bought me a stone bird, a candle, and a packet of herbs that I use in cooking.

★**Handmade cards.** My grandchild makes cards for me, writing his own verses inside. He tells me that he likes the warm rooms, the apple pies, and the nice smells at my house. I appreciate his thoughts and, of course, I have saved all the cards.

★**Jewelry.** I remember a jewelry box that a young admirer hand-crafted for me. It is about 18 inches high, painted an antique yellow. The clasp and hinges were beaten to give them the antiqued look. The work and caring that went into this creation were gifts in themselves.

61

★**Ring.** My grandmother gave me an opal ring in an heirloom setting. She had picked out a new stone. It was the first feminine thing I received.

★**Weekend.** My four children got together and arranged for my husband and me to spend a weekend at a hotel with dinner. It was all taken care of. At first, I couldn't believe it, and I didn't want to leave. We had a wonderful time because of their thoughtfulness.

★**Needlepoint.** My daughter-in-law needlepointed a pattern for me, saying that she was glad to have a mother-in-law who was also a friend. It is now hanging in my home.

★**Love.** My mother wrapped a small, empty box for me. She tied it with a number of beautiful bows. I could tell how much of her time and effort she put into the result. The accompanying note said that this was not to be opened, as it contained a bit of her. Whenever I have

62

been down or depressed, I take the box out and know that it contains Mom's love. This small, well-wrapped box has been displayed on my shelf for years.

★ **Engagement ring.** When I graduated from college I got a particularly wonderful gift from my mother. It was the engagement ring that my father, who had since passed away, had given to her.

★ **Binoculars.** A special friend and I have had a number of good, long conversations about seeing things clearly in our lives, about setting goals for ourselves. Later, and for no special occasion, this friend sent me a gift of fine binoculars. He didn't have to explain; I knew that it was one way he could make certain that I would see my world clearly. I take them with me whenever I travel. I even use them on airplanes.

63

★ **Stepladder**. I know this sounds like a strange gift, and I thought so at the time. However, my brother gave it to me, and I have found it to be one of the most used gifts that I have ever had. I use it when I hang pictures, when I paint, and so on. It is old, ugly, paint-spattered, and an essential favorite.

★ **Picture frame**. One Valentine's Day, my husband spent hours working on his gift for me. He had made a frame for a picture of the two of us. The frame incorporated wood from our home in Montana, crystals, and a large heart-shaped stone. There was a ledge at the bottom of the frame for me to display special items. I love it because it is *of* us and made *by* him.

★ **Video**. Some friends of mine made a video about me for one of my special birthdays. The video was so perfect and so hilarious that it was shown more than once at my birthday party. It was the story of my life, with

64

a doll representing me shown flying over the country, represented by a map; in a bush, representing the Northwest; etc. A real hit. Totally personal.

★ **Papaya**. My husband and I were married in Hawaii in January. When Christmas came, I was planning to fill my stocking and his, but he told me that he would take care of mine. On Christmas morning my stocking was bulging. On the very top there was a fresh papaya—a memory of our wedding and a favorite fruit of mine.

★ **Photo album**. My mom spent hours with her family photo albums. From them she created a new album, filled with pictures of just me that she gave to me on my birthday. Pictures of me from the time she was pregnant, up to my wedding, and even after that. She had the cover quilted, then placed a picture of Mom and two-year-old me, together on the cover.

★ **Pin**. I have a close and active relationship with a group of four other women. We do a lot of wonderful and silly things together. One of these women gave me a pin, a silver pin of five people standing arm in arm. This is a striking and lovely representation of who we are to each other.

★ **Dirt bike**. It's fun! It's something that I do with my dad.

★ **Photo album**. On our Golden Anniversary, each of our guests filled a page of a photo album with personal memories, notes, momentos, and photos, and brought it to the party. These pages were assembled in a specially prepared cover and were given to us to look through at our leisure. I don't know what could have been better.

★**Plants**. Over two years ago my father passed away. Some people sent plants rather than flowers. The plants are still growing.

66

★ **Painting.** I spent some time touring with an artist and his wife. During this time, he painted a number of pictures. One of the paintings was special to me, and we talked about it. Later, this elderly man was visiting my city. He brought me the same painting, presenting it as a gift. Not only did I appreciate the gift itself, but also his effort of carrying it with him on the plane and up several flights of stairs to my apartment.

★ **Picture.** As a professional speaker, I have had many gifts given to me after presentations and many photographs taken of me. One gift combined the two. After a presentation with a technology theme, I received a picture of me giving my speech. The frame had a device which recorded the first 10 seconds of my talk. I can play and replay how I sounded when I was on the very platform pictured. It was a gift that beautifully blended the personal, the event, and the technical.

★ **Bikini.** When I was a 15-year-old girl, I had lots of friends but no dates. I was late developing, and nobody seemed to take my internal feelings seriously. When I moved with my parents to California at this age, my mother, sensitive to my feelings, gave me two things: baby doll pajamas and a bikini. The first day I arrived at our new home and wore the bikini, a boy talked to me on the beach. Her gift helped me to bridge the important gap between being everyone's friend and being a girl someone wanted to date.

★ **Flowers**. There have been days when work has been stressful. Days when I feel abused. My husband cares that I am having a bad day, he loves me, he thinks I am wonderful, and he is there for me. He will let me know this by sending me a bouquet of flowers while I am still at my desk.

★ **Bracelet.** My late grandmother gave my mother a golden bracelet to pass on

68

to me for my dowry. It has great senti-
mental value to me, and I wear it now,
even though I have not married.

★ **Paper piano.** I love gifts that are
honest and come deep from the heart.
As a piano teacher I used to tell my
students, "You move to another class,
but I stay here." But one of my students
came back. He waited outside the staff
room for a long time. When I appeared,
he gave me a small piano that he had
created from folded paper. He was only
7 or 8 years old. He gave it to me and
said nothing, but we both knew that this
was important.

★ **Handpainted cards.** A student
painted three different cards for me.
They all featured hearts: a red heart, a
semi-dark one, and a dark one. He told
me that the red heart was my heart, as
I was a loving teacher.

★ **Painting.** A master in my life was a
calligrapher. Shortly before his death,

he created and framed one of his works for me, presenting it to me before a large group.

★ **Pewter lamp.** My husband gave me a small, 10" hammered pewter lamp. I use it for reading year-round, even in the summer, when it's not very dark.

★ **Mantle.** Our fireplace needed a mantle after we had covered the wall with rock. A friend of ours said that he would like to make one and give it to us. We love it, although after six years of waiting for it, we had grown rather attached to the hole we had left for it!

★**Champagne and cookbook.** For our wedding, we received a gift that spoiled us for the rest of our lives. It was a bottle of fine French champagne and a French cookbook. We were not "into" either of them before. Now we are, and we have given the same gift to other newlyweds, even though it is necessary to trace the now-out-of-print book.

70

★ **Cruise.** My daughter gave me a cruise that we took together. A week sailing the Inside Passage to Alaska, revisiting where she lived and went to kindergarten.

★ **Roses.** Our first anniversary, my husband and I were apart. Our second anniversary, there was very little money, so my husband gave me two long-stemmed red roses. Every year after that, I have received a bouquet of long-stemmed red roses— one for each year.

★ **Necklace.** A young woman who has been like a daughter to me gave me, on my birthday, a four-strand necklace of black onyx pearls. I was overwhelmed and, for the first time in my life, speechless.

★ **Dinner.** One Mother's Day when I was alone, a couple I knew asked me to go out to dinner. I would have been content to be by myself, but I

71

recognized their thoughtfulness in thinking that I should have someone to celebrate me on this particular day.

★ **Certificates.** I love to get certificates from my children and grandchildren. Good for cleaning the bathroom, mowing the grass, pulling weeds. I know they are thinking and giving of themselves.

★ **Certificates.** My children used to give me certificates to do things around the house. That was 25 years ago. I guess I should start cashing them in.

★ **Babysitting.** One of the best gifts that I received at a baby shower was a note that was good for four nights of babysitting. I loved knowing that my baby would be cared for when I went out.

★ **Wine.** I received a surprise from a couple I had invited to use my washer and dryer rather than go to a laundro-

72

mat. I had expected nothing, yet they gave me a case of very good wine.

★ **Transportation.** I took my granddaughter on a trip to Disneyland. When we returned, it was late, and my mind was on getting a cab home. To my delight, some friends were at the airport to take us home, even though it was two in the morning.

★ **Flowers.** My Mother's Day flowers came from my daughter a week before the actual Sunday, because she knew that I would be going out of town the day after Mother's Day. This gave me a whole week to enjoy them.

★ **My husband.** My husband of 56 years has always been my love, my thoughtful love. He dedicated his book to me.

★ **Rings.** It seemed to be the time to wrap up my rings, which had been a family legacy, and present them lovingly to my daughter. She received them

tearfully and happily, and I have had the joy of watching her wear them. Then, as a total surprise, my husband picked out another ring, a diamond ring, to replace what I had passed along. When we were married, we had no money for a "proper" engagement ring, so this one was very special.

★ **Autobiography.** Every Christms Eve the entire family, including children and grandchildren, traditionally gathers at the home of my parents. Dad reads *The Night Before Christmas* to all of us. This year, before the reading, he gave each of us a book that he had written and Mom had wrapped. It was his autobiography, and he had printed copies for each of us.

★**A letter.** I received a letter from a woman when her father died. I was a minister for many years, and she was the first child I baptized. When her mother passed away, I was with her. My wife and I were the first callers after

74

this death. I had retired by the time her father passed away, but at her request I assisted at his funeral. The letter from her said that one of the greatest gifts that her parents had given to her was the gift of knowing the two of us. We had not known that we meant that much to her.

★ **A poem.** The one I remember is one that my husband wrote to me for my birthday. It brought tears to my eyes.

★ **Macramé holder.** This gift was a surprise to me and particularly special, because it was made by my 10-year-old godchild.

★ **Money.** I was in dire need and reluctantly asked a friend if she had $100 that she could loan me. Her gift to me was much more than the $100 I asked for. She had been putting this money aside and convinced me that she would feel much better giving it to me than spending it somewhere else. It

75

would give her much pleasure. She would not consider it a loan but a gift.

★ **Invitation.** When we got married, the first gift that we unwrapped was one of our most special gifts. It was our wedding invitation, beautifully framed.

★ **Video.** My sister gave me a birthday gift of a video, beginning with a scene of her in a garden. It was shot with a diffused filter, which made it look as though she were thinking. In the garden, she was mentally writing a letter to me, remembering all of the things that we had done together and been to one another. Her voice came through loud and clear, and the video was interspersed with photos that were connected to the memories. There was not a dry eye in the room while we watched.

★ **Nightgown.** A friend of many years made a nightgown for me of very fine cotton and heavy smocking around the

76

neck and sleeves. We had done so many different things together that this gift was special, because of the time and skill involved. I was honored to receive it.

★ **Flowers.** I had always said that I didn't want flowers, because they were expensive and they died. My husband had never sent them before, so I was totally surprised when I received a large bouquet of 26 pink and yellow roses for an anniversary. He sent them to my office, and I absolutely loved them.

★ **Thank you card.** My oldest son, 29, recently sent me a number of thank you cards. He had written a note to me on each of them. They mean a lot to me.

77

Giving

★ **Crocheted items.** When I give gifts to someone special, I like to give them something that I have crocheted. The doilies and sachets take a lot of time. It means a lot to me, to give something that I have invested my own self in.

★ **Baskets**. I like to give baskets (and cross-stitched things I make) to my family, because I love them—both the family and the baskets.

★**Memories.** Whenever I do something wonderful, I will buy a gift for myself as a personal reward. I can always re-member what the reason was for each item.

★**Support.** We support a child in Ecuador through World Vision.

★**Time.** Giving time to be together. This is what has the greatest personal value.

78

★**Organ.** Give an organ. Be an organ donor.

★**Love.** The best things you can give are love, consideration, kindness and thoughtfulness. Everything else stems from them.

79

THE NITTY GRITTY
OF GIFT GIVING

This list of motifs and hobbies is not for an instant to be considered complete. Its purpose is to jump start your own list of ideas for the people you will give to. You can begin your brainstorming with these lists and go from there.

81

Motifs, interests, and Collections

What does this person love to talk about—fishing or birdwatching? Music or gourmet food? Give him or her a present concerning a favorite subject, such as:

Music boxes. Duck decoys. Swans. Spoons. Monet. Pelicans. Camels. Fans. Sunflowers. Cats. Paisley. Bunnies. Wild West. Santas. Shells. Mugs. Toy trains. Wristwatches. Apples. Teapots. Angels. Butterflies. Dolls. Candle holders. Elephants.

More?

82

Hobbies

- ★ **Gardening.** Herbs. Flowers. Veggies. Tools. Books. Shoes. Garden stakes. Plants. Gloves. Seeds. Magazines. Pots. Hats. Shoes. Statues. Row markers.
- ★ **Sports.** Clothes. Equipment. Fanny pack. Socks. Insignia on clothing. Carry bags. Water bottle.
- ★ **Reading.** Books by favorite author. Dictionary stand. Book for collections (first editions, etc.). Fancy bookmarks. Bookstands. Reading lamp. Glasses holder. Reading pillow.
- ★ **Woodworking.** Tools. Videos. Masks. Toolcases. Hanging shelves. Miter box. Clamps. Chisels. Vises. Eye and ear protectors. Gloves. Measuring devises. Tuition for special classes. Glue. Oils. Magazine subscription. Books.

★ **Mechanics.** Wrenches. Trolley. Strong hand cleaner. Toolbox. Stacking bins for organization. Shop vacuum. Overalls. Magazine subscription. Book. High quality tools. Heavy-duty extension cords. Videos.

★ **Music.** Certificate for a tape or CD every month. Carrying case. Music of favorite artist. Concert tickets. CD or tape cleaner. Storage racks.

★ **Wine.** Equipment. A special vintage. Magazine subscription. Wine racks. Corkscrews. Glass-ware. Wine preservation devices. Decanter. Drip tray. Book. Wine-related T-shirts. Poster. Map. Wine rack.

What are some other hobbies and related gift ideas?

84

Feel free to duplicate the SIZE CHART and FASHION SURVEYS on the following pages. Fill them out with current information for those on your gift list. Take the charts with you on shopping trips, to feel confident that you will make some Perfect Gift choices.

85

★ ★ ★ ★ ★ ★ ★ ★ ★ ★ ★ ★

SIZE CHART FOR HER

_____

(Name)

Child   S M L XL

Adult   S M L XL (circle one)

Blouse	_____	Sweater	_____
Slacks	_____	Shorts	_____
Shoes	_____	Pants	_____
Socks	_____	Tanktop	_____
Nylons	_____	T-shirts	_____
Hat	_____	Sweats	_____
Ring	_____	Sleep	
Belt	_____	wear	_____
Gloves	_____	Jacket	_____
Dress	_____	More:	_____

_____

_____

86

★ ★ ★ ★ ★ ★ ★ ★ ★ ★ ★ ★

SIZE CHART FOR HIM

_____

(Name)

Child   S M L XL
Adult   S M L XL (circle one)

Shirt	_____	Sweater	_____
Pants	_____	Shorts	_____
Shoes	_____	Pants	_____
Socks	_____	Tanktop	_____
Hat	_____	T-shirts	_____
Gloves	_____	Sweats	_____
Belt	_____	Sleep	
Ring	_____	wear	_____
Jacket	_____	More:	_____

_____

_____

_____

87

FASHION SURVEY
(BEFORE BUYING FOR *HER*, FIND OUT WHAT SHE REALLY LIKES.)

Name _____

Circle whatever is appropriate:

KNIT TOPS

Styles:

Tanks

T-shirts

Sweaters

Vest

Cardigan

Sleeveless

Long sleeves

Short sleeves

Colors:

Patterns:

Stripes

Solids

Multi-colored

88

DRESSES

Length:
Short
Mini
Knee
Calf
Full
Tea

Fabric:
Heavy
Silky
Cotton
Synthetic
Natural

Style:
Tailored
Coatdress
Jumper
Belted
Loose
Two-piece
Evening

Colors:

89

BLOUSES

Neckline:

Jewel

V-shaped

Cowl

Turtleneck

Boatneck

Collared

Style:

Conservative

Daring

Long sleeves

Short sleeves

Worn alone or
  under jackets

Over turtlenecks or
  other knit shirts

Worn open or closed

Buttoned in front or back

Fabric:

Silky

Cotton

Synthetic

Natural

Patterns:

Plain-colored

Geometric designs

Floral prints

Colors:

90

SKIRTS

Fabric:

Heavy

Light

Flowing

Wool

Pattern:

Cotton

Solid-color

Tweed

Plaid

Checked

Geometric

Style:

Full

Fitted

Pleated

Straight

Tulip

A-line

Wrap

Colors:

Length:

Above the knee

Mini

Knee length

Mid-calf

JACKETS

Pattern:
Solid
Floral
Geometric
Style:
Open
Buttoned
Casual
Drawstring
Loose
Fitted
Short
Long

Fabric:
Heavy
Light
Linen
Synthetic
Wool
Gabardine
Silk
Leather
Denim

Colors:

92

SLACKS

Style:

Full-length

Knee-length

Elastic waist

Fitted

Front-pleated

Non-pleated

Cuffed

Other:

Colors:

Pattern:

Solid-colored

Print

Geometric

Tweed

Fabric:

Heavy

Light

Linen

Synthetic

Wool

Gabardine

Silk

Leather

93

SHOES

Evening shoes:

Gold

Silver

Clear

Fabric

Daytime:

Pumps

Flats

Sports

Casual

Sandals

Slippers

Colors:

(Note: This is a good place to record basic wardrobe colors)

Boots:

Winter

Cowboy

Rain

Fleece

Gardening

Fashion

94

STOCKINGS

Nylons:

Pantyhose
Gartered
Knee-high
Plain
Textured
Patterned

Socks:

Ankle
Slouchy
Patterned
Whimsical

Colors:

HATS

Style:

Fashion statement
Sunshade
Natural straw
Felt
Tie down
Brim
Beret
Turban
Jungle

Colors:

Trim for an existing hat:

Flower
Scarf
Pin
Feathers

96

BELTS

Colors:

Narrow
Medium
Wide
Basic color
Metallic
Fashion

SCARVES

Shape:
Oblong
Square

Use:

In pocket

Around neck

Around shoulders

Around a hat

Over a coat

Fashion statement

With an outfit

Colors:

97

GLOVES

Long

Short

Leather

Patterned

Lined

Colors:

JEWELRY

Pins:

Metal

Ceramic

Gemstone

Motif

Earrings:

Pierced

Clip

Daytime

Evening

Favorite gemstone:

Favorite metal:

Gold

Silver

Type:

Costume

Fine

Bracelets:

Bangle

Clasp

Colored

Metal

Rings:

Cocktail

Everyday

Necklaces:

Choker

Chains

Pearls

98

COLORS
    Favorites:

    Won't wear:

OUTFITS
    Preferences:

    Colors:

SEPARATES
    Preferences:

    Colors:

99

FASHION SURVEY
(BEFORE BUYING FOR *HIM,* FIND OUT WHAT HE REALLY LIKES.)

Name

PANTS

Fabric:

Heavy

Light

Circle
whatever
is
appropriate

Wrinkles okay

Front-pleated

Non-pleated

Cuffs

Pattern:

Solid

Geometric

Colors:

Checks

Stripes

Tweed

100

SHIRTS

Collar:
Open
Closed
Button-down
Special

Style:
Traditional
Bold
Solid
Prints

Fabric:
Silk
Cotton
Blend
Percale
Oxford cloth
Wash and wear

Sleeves:
Long
Short
Rolled up
French cuffs

Casual:
Knit cuffs and collar
T-shirt
Worn alone
Under jacket

Colors:

101

JACKETS

Pattern:

Tweed

Plain

Plaid

Herringbone

Style:

Single-breasted

Double-breasted

Single vent

Double vent

Suit

Casual

Sport

Outdoor

Fabric:

Heavy

Light

Natural

Leather

Synthetic

Colors:

102

HATS

Use and Style:

Baseball

Fishing

Golf

Skiing

Hiking

Cowboy

Beret

Colors:

RING

Material:

Silver

Gold

Other metal:

Style:

Stones:

Insignia:

103

SWEATERS

Fabric:
Cotton
Wool
Other

Style:
Thin
Bulky
Oversized
Patterned
Plain
Vest
Cardigan

Specific design:

Motif:

Colors:

104

COATS

Pattern:

Geometric

Tweed

Solid

Fabric:

Waterproof

Denim

Wool

Leather

Style:

Hooded

Belted

Raglan

Single-breasted

Double-breasted

Length:

Long

Knee-length

Short jacket

Colors:

105

SHOES

Shoes:

Dress
Casual
Work
Sport
Outdoor
Boat
Slippers

Boots:

Colors:

Hiking
Fishing
Gardening
Outdoor

106

COLORS
> **Favorites:**

> **Avoid:**

OUTFITS
> **Preferences:**

> **Colors:**

SEPARATES
> **Preferences:**

> **Colors:**

107

GIFT IDEAS FOR *HER*

Clothing:

T-shirt and sweatshirt
Scarf (wool or silk) and gloves
    (wool or leather)
Robe, pajamas, and
    slippers
Exercise clothes
Belts with inter-
    changeable buckles
Jacket, hat, and vest
Tank top and shorts
Lingerie

Other:

Non-Clothing:

Suitcase with plane tickets inside
Wristwatch for fashion accent
Travel coffee mug and pound of
    gourmet coffee

108

Tote bag and exercise video

Wallet or coin purse and purse with money tucked inside

Umbrella (motif)

Mirror

Hair accessories —clips, bows, headbands

Jewelry chest and earring holder

Perfume, cologne, and powder in cosmetic bag

Plant or floating flowers

Shoe decorations and clips

Stuffed animal

Bouquet of flowers

Addition to an existing collection

Chef's apron, placemats, and napkins

Beach bag, beach towel, visor, and plastic water bottle with straw

Hats in decorated hat boxes

Sachet and soaps
Candles
Wine glasses

110

GIFT IDEAS FOR *HIM*

Clothing

Shirt, tie, and sweater
Jacket, hat, and scarf
Silk boxer shorts,
    nightshirt, and robe
Sandals and bathing suit
Hiking boots and wool socks
T-shirt and sweatshirt with logo of
    favorite team
Cravat or bow tie, belt and
    scarf
Cummerbund and tie set
Monogrammed
    dress shirt

Non-Clothing:

Wallet with money
    enclosed
Picture in silver frame
Brandy and snifters

111

Holder for eye glasses

Shoe accessories—polish, waterproofing, brushes

Manicure kit

Sports bag with sports accessories enclosed

Pen set, stationery, and stamps

Travelling game

Portable laptop computer and computer game

Umbrella

Attaché

Sunglasses, beach towel, and plane tickets in carry-all bag

Suspenders

Cufflinks

Business card case with key chain or key case

Metal collar stays and tie pin

Baseball cap and tickets to baseball game

Cologne and after shave in toilet kit

Microbrew beer and mugs

Travel coffee mug
Gourmet coffee and espresso
  machine

113

GIFT IDEAS FOR *BOTH* OR *EITHER*

Wine coaster or container
Marble cutting board with knives
Hurricane lamp
Long matches in
    brass container
Big bowl for ice cream
Mugs—packed with
    chocolate-covered
    espresso beans
Potpourri in vase
Down comforter and books
Address book and calendar with
    favorite theme
Birdhouse and sundial
Candles and candleholder
Shower curtain and
    matching towels
Holiday decorations
Extra special bottle of wine
Art work—painting, photo,
    sculpture, lithograph

114

Board game, playing cards, and card table

Gourmet candy in clear container

Video with popcorn

Tickets for concerts, classes, sports, etc.

115

GIFT BRAINSTORM

Use these circles to brainstorm what you would like to give friends and relatives.

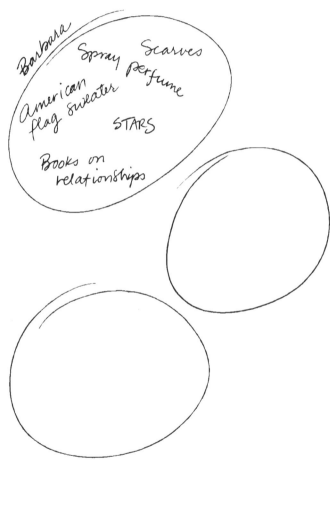

Barbara

Spray   Scarves

American
flag sweater   perfume

STARS

Books on
relationships

116

GIFT RECORD FOR

_____
(Name)

Reminders of gifts you've given this person recently, as well as ideas for future gifts.

_____
(Year)
Birthday_____
Valentine_____
Christmas_____
Other_____

_____
(Year)
Birthday_____
Valentine_____
Christmas_____
Other_____

117

_____
 (Year)
Birthday_____
Valentine_____
Christmas_____
Other_____

_____
 (Year)
Birthday_____
Valentine_____
Christmas_____
Other_____

_____
 (Year)
Birthday_____
Valentine_____
Christmas_____
Other_____

118

ORDER FORM

Qty.	Title	Price	Can.Price	Total
	Giving the Perfect Gift	$8.95	$10.95	
	Subtotal			
	Shipping and Handling (add $3.00 for one book, $2.00 for each additional book)			
	Sales tax (WA residents only, add 8.2%)			
	Total enclosed			

Telephone Orders:
Call 1-800-468-1994.
Have your VISA or
Mastercard ready.

FAX Orders:
1-206-745-0992. Fill out
order blank and fax.

Postal Orders:
Perfect Gift
P.O. Box 13006
Mill Creek, WA 98012

Payment: Please Check One:

☐ **Check**

☐ **VISA**

☐ **MasterCard**

Expiration Date:_____/_____
Card #:_____
Name on Card:_____

NAME_____

ADDRESS_____

CITY_____**STATE**_____**ZIP**_____

DAYTIME PHONE_____

Quantity discounts are available.
For more information, call 206-672-8597.
Thank you for your order!
You may return any books for a full refund if not satisfied.
Sandy is available for keynotes and workshops. (206 485-4855).

119